´FOOTBALL
TEMPLATES
SPECIAL TEAMS´

English edition

JAVIER ADAME

FOOTBALL TEMPLATES

SPECIAL TEAMS

Author:

Gustavo Javier Adame Guajardo

ISBN: 9798741098998

Independently published

First edition: June 2021

Monterrey, Nuevo León

MÉXICO

Printed in the United States of America

"THE SUPPORT OF QUALITY STANDARDS
IN THE SPECIAL TEAMS UNIT
WILL GIVE US A GREATER CHANCE OF
SUCCESS IN THE DIFFERENT
SITUATIONS THAT MAY OCCUR
DURING A GAME."

-HC Javier Adame

I DEDICATE THIS BOOK FOOTBALL TEMPLATES SPECIAL TEAMS TO ALL READERS OF MY PREVIOUS BOOKS, HOPING TO BE OF GREAT HELP FOR THE PRACTICE AND LEARNING OF FOOTBALL.

INDEX

CONTENT

The following formats will help you better organize and structure during special team practice.

The tools shown in this book will be indispensable for special team coordinators and support coaches.

1)DIAGRAMS, SPECIAL TEMS PERSONNEL FILLING IN:

In this structure you can give a better stay to the player staff of each special unit, making it easier for the coach to organize them.

2)DIAGRAMS, DRAWING FORMATIONS-COVERAGES AND ADJUSTMENTS PUNT KICK:

The formations and coverage adjustments are highlighted against the attack patterns in the opposing teams scout.

3)DIAGRAMAS, DRAWING PLAYS PUNT RETURN:

It is important to divide the plays in this special team by the quantity of returners.

4)DIAGRAMS, EVALUATION FILLING IN PUNT RE-TURNERS:

A filling in table is displayed for daily evaluation of returners, it is recommended to work with 3 returners daily, in order to achieve the highest quantity of repetitions.

5)DIAGRAMS, DRAWING PLAYS KO:

It is important to include our moves by showing the indicated direction of the kick.

6)DIAGRAMS, DRAWING PLAYS KO RETURN:

It is important to divide our plays by the quantity of players and formations we have on our returns.

7)DIAGRAMS, EVALUATION FILLING IN FG & KO KICKERS:

It recommends to work 2 days during the week, alternating the number of daily kicks.

8)DIAGRAMS, EVALUATION FILLING IN PUNT & 120 KICKERS:

It recommends to work 2 days during the week, alternating the number of daily kicks.

9)DIAGRAMS, DRAWING PLAYS AND ADJUSTMENTS FG:

It is recommended to work special coverages and plays for at least five minutes during each practice.

10)DIAGRAMS, DRAWING PLAYS AND ADJUSTMENTS FG BLOCK:

It is recommended to work special coverages and plays for at least five minutes during each practice.

END:

Latest comments related to the football templates special teams workbook.

ABOUT THE AUTHOR:

Data concerning the author and his work philosophy.

INTRODUCTION

The structure of this book consists of the elaboration of templates or sheets with diagrams, with correspond to the plays during the moments of planning, practices or quality control statistic which is carried within a professional, college or high school staff.

This workbook will help you have more tools which you can support yourself for supervision and correction during practice periods.

1

SPECIAL TEAMS PERSONNEL

_____
_____
_____
_____
_____
_____
_____
_____
_____
_____
_____
_____
_____
_____
_____
_____
_____
_____
_____
_____
_____
_____
_____
_____
_____
_____
_____
_____
_____
_____
_____

PERSONNEL BY UNIT
SPECIAL TEAMS

PUNT

R1	LWB	LT	LG	CENTER	RG	RT	RWB	R1

KICKER	PROTECH

PUNT RETURN

1	2	3	4	5	6	7	8

LCB	RETURNERS	LCB

KICK OFF COVERAGE

L1	L2	L3	L4	L5	R5	R4	R3	R2	R1

KICKER

KICK OFF RETURN

LT	LG	CENTER	RG	RT

L1	HANDS	BB BK	HANDS	R1

LRET	HANDS	MIDDLE RT	HANDS	RRT

PAT & FG BLOCK

1	2	3	4	5	6	7	8	9	10	11

PERSONNEL BY UNIT
SPECIAL TEAMS

PUNT

R1	LWB	LT	LG	CENTER	RG	RT	RWB	R1

KICKER	PROTECH

PUNT RETURN

1	2	3	4	5	6	7	8

LCB	RETURNERS	LCB

KICK OFF COVERAGE

L1	L2	L3	L4	L5	R5	R4	R3	R2	R1

KICKER

KICK OFF RETURN

LT	LG	CENTER	RG	RT

L1	HANDS	BB BK	HANDS	R1

LRET	HANDS	MIDDLE RT	HANDS	RRT

PAT & FG BLOCK

1	2	3	4	5	6	7	8	9	10	11

PERSONNEL BY UNIT
SPECIAL TEAMS

PUNT

R1	LWB	LT	LG	CENTER	RG	RT	RWB	R1

KICKER	PROTECH

PUNT RETURN

1	2	3	4	5	6	7	8

LCB	RETURNERS	LCB

KICK OFF COVERAGE

L1	L2	L3	L4	L5	R5	R4	R3	R2	R1

KICKER

KICK OFF RETURN

LT	LG	CENTER	RG	RT

L1	HANDS	BB BK	HANDS	R1

LRET	HANDS	MIDDLE RT	HANDS	RRT

PAT & FG BLOCK

1	2	3	4	5	6	7	8	9	10	11

PERSONNEL BY UNIT
SPECIAL TEAMS

PUNT

R1	LWB	LT	LG	CENTER	RG	RT	RWB	R1

KICKER	PROTECH

PUNT RETURN

1	2	3	4	5	6	7	8

LCB	RETURNERS	LCB

KICK OFF COVERAGE

L1	L2	L3	L4	L5	R5	R4	R3	R2	R1

KICKER

KICK OFF RETURN

LT	LG	CENTER	RG	RT

L1	HANDS	BB BK	HANDS	R1

LRET	HANDS	MIDDLE RT	HANDS	RRT

PAT & FG BLOCK

1	2	3	4	5	6	7	8	9	10	11

PERSONNEL BY UNIT
SPECIAL TEAMS

PUNT

R1	LWB	LT	LG	CENTER	RG	RT	RWB	R1

KICKER	PROTECH

PUNT RETURN

1	2	3	4	5	6	7	8

LCB	RETURNERS	LCB

KICK OFF COVERAGE

L1	L2	L3	L4	L5	R5	R4	R3	R2	R1

KICKER

KICK OFF RETURN

LT	LG	CENTER	RG	RT

L1	HANDS	BB BK	HANDS	R1

LRET	HANDS	MIDDLE RT	HANDS	RRT

PAT & FG BLOCK

1	2	3	4	5	6	7	8	9	10	11

PERSONNEL BY UNIT
SPECIAL TEAMS

PUNT

R1	LWB	LT	LG	CENTER	RG	RT	RWB	R1

KICKER	PROTECH

PUNT RETURN

1	2	3	4	5	6	7	8

LCB	RETURNERS	LCB

KICK OFF COVERAGE

L1	L2	L3	L4	L5	R5	R4	R3	R2	R1

KICKER

KICK OFF RETURN

LT	LG	CENTER	RG	RT

L1	HANDS	BB BK	HANDS	R1

LRET	HANDS	MIDDLE RT	HANDS	RRT

PAT & FG BLOCK

1	2	3	4	5	6	7	8	9	10	11

PERSONNEL BY UNIT
SPECIAL TEAMS

PUNT

R1	LWB	LT	LG	CENTER	RG	RT	RWB	R1

KICKER	PROTECH

PUNT RETURN

1	2	3	4	5	6	7	8

LCB	RETURNERS	LCB

KICK OFF COVERAGE

L1	L2	L3	L4	L5	R5	R4	R3	R2	R1

KICKER

KICK OFF RETURN

LT	LG	CENTER	RG	RT

L1	HANDS	BB BK	HANDS	R1

LRET	HANDS	MIDDLE RT	HANDS	RRT

PAT & FG BLOCK

1	2	3	4	5	6	7	8	9	10	11

PERSONNEL BY UNIT
SPECIAL TEAMS

PUNT

R1	LWB	LT	LG	CENTER	RG	RT	RWB	R1

KICKER	PROTECH

PUNT RETURN

1	2	3	4	5	6	7	8

LCB	RETURNERS	LCB

KICK OFF COVERAGE

L1	L2	L3	L4	L5	R5	R4	R3	R2	R1

KICKER

KICK OFF RETURN

LT	LG	CENTER	RG	RT

L1	HANDS	BB BK	HANDS	R1

LRET	HANDS	MIDDLE RT	HANDS	RRT

PAT & FG BLOCK

1	2	3	4	5	6	7	8	9	10	11

PERSONNEL BY UNIT
SPECIAL TEAMS

PUNT

R1	LWB	LT	LG	CENTER	RG	RT	RWB	R1

KICKER	PROTECH

PUNT RETURN

1	2	3	4	5	6	7	8

LCB	RETURNERS	LCB

KICK OFF COVERAGE

L1	L2	L3	L4	L5	R5	R4	R3	R2	R1

KICKER

KICK OFF RETURN

LT	LG	CENTER	RG	RT

L1	HANDS	BB BK	HANDS	R1

LRET	HANDS	MIDDLE RT	HANDS	RRT

PAT & FG BLOCK

1	2	3	4	5	6	7	8	9	10	11

PERSONNEL BY UNIT
SPECIAL TEAMS

PUNT

R1	LWB	LT	LG	CENTER	RG	RT	RWB	R1

KICKER	PRO TECH

PUNT RETURN

1	2	3	4	5	6	7	8

LCB	RETURNERS	LCB

KICK OFF COVERAGE

L1	L2	L3	L4	L5	R5	R4	R3	R2	R1

KICKER

KICK OFF RETURN

LT	LG	CENTER	RG	RT

L1	HANDS	BB BK	HANDS	R1

LRET	HANDS	MIDDLE RT	HANDS	RRT

PAT & FG BLOCK

1	2	3	4	5	6	7	8	9	10	11

NOTES

2

PUNT KICK
FORMATIONS AND
ANDJUSTMENTS

_____
_____
_____
_____
_____
_____
_____
_____
_____
_____
_____
_____
_____
_____
_____
_____
_____
_____
_____
_____
_____
_____
_____
_____
_____
_____
_____
_____
_____
_____
_____

PUNT
FORMATIONS:

_____
_____
_____

ADJUSTMENTS :

_____
_____
_____
_____
_____
_____
_____
_____
_____

PUNT
FORMATIONS:

ADJUSTMENTS :

PUNT
FORMATIONS:

_____
_____
_____

ADJUSTMENTS :

_____
_____
_____
_____
_____
_____
_____
_____
_____
_____

PUNT
FORMATIONS:

_____
_____
_____

ADJUSTMENTS :

_____
_____
_____
_____
_____
_____
_____
_____
_____

PUNT
FORMATIONS:

ADJUSTMENTS :

PUNT
FORMATIONS:

ADJUSTMENTS :

PUNT
FORMATIONS:

ADJUSTMENTS :

PUNT
FORMATIONS:

_____

_____

_____

ADJUSTMENTS :

_____

_____

_____

_____

_____

_____

_____

_____

_____

PUNT
FORMATIONS:

_____

_____

_____

ADJUSTMENTS :

_____
_____
_____
_____
_____
_____
_____
_____
_____

PUNT
FORMATIONS:

_____
_____
_____

ADJUSTMENTS :

_____
_____
_____
_____
_____
_____
_____
_____
_____
_____

PUNT
FORMATIONS:

ADJUSTMENTS :

PUNT
FORMATIONS:

ADJUSTMENTS :

PUNT
FORMATIONS:

ADJUSTMENTS :

_____
_____
_____
_____
_____
_____
_____
_____
_____

PUNT
FORMATIONS:

ADJUSTMENTS :

PUNT
FORMATIONS:

ADJUSTMENTS :

PUNT
FORMATIONS:

_____

_____

_____

_____

ADJUSTMENTS :

_____

_____

_____

_____

_____

_____

_____

_____

_____

_____

PUNT
FORMATIONS:

_____
_____
_____

ADJUSTMENTS :

_____
_____
_____
_____
_____
_____
_____
_____
_____
_____

PUNT
FORMATIONS:

ADJUSTMENTS :

PUNT
FORMATIONS:

ADJUSTMENTS :

PUNT
FORMATIONS:

_____
_____
_____

ADJUSTMENTS :

_____
_____
_____
_____
_____
_____
_____
_____
_____
_____

NOTES

_____
_____
_____
_____
_____
_____
_____
_____
_____
_____
_____
_____
_____
_____
_____
_____
_____
_____
_____
_____
_____
_____
_____
_____
_____
_____
_____
_____
_____
_____
_____
_____
_____
_____
_____
_____
_____

PUNT RETURN PLAYS

3

_____

_____

_____

_____

_____

_____

_____

_____

_____

_____

_____

_____

_____

_____

_____

_____

_____

_____

_____

_____

_____

_____

_____

_____

_____

_____

_____

_____

_____

_____

_____

_____

_____

PUNT RETURN PLAYS:

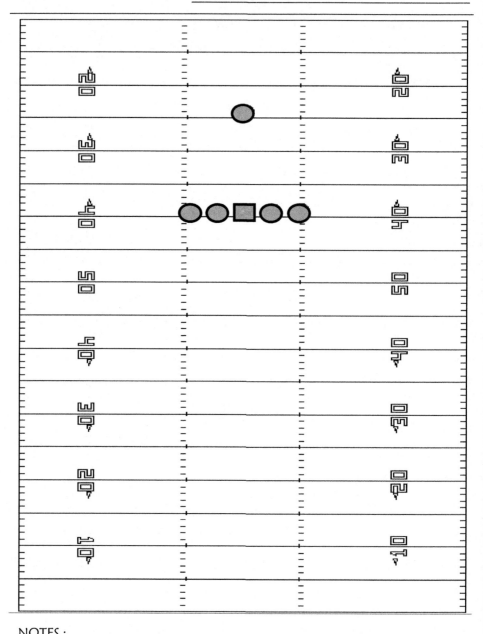

NOTES :

PUNT RETURN
PLAYS:

_____

_____

_____

NOTES :

_____

_____

_____

_____

PUNT RETURN
PLAYS:

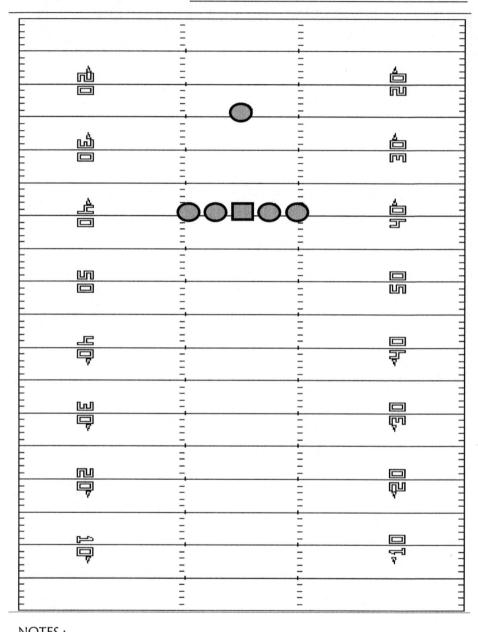

NOTES :

PUNT RETURN PLAYS:

NOTES :

PUNT RETURN
PLAYS:

_____
_____
_____

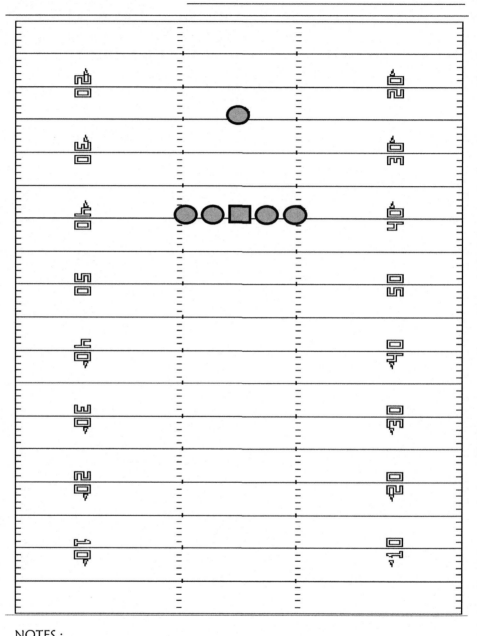

NOTES :

_____
_____
_____
_____

PUNT RETURN PLAYS:

NOTES :

_____
_____
_____
_____

PUNT RETURN
PLAYS:

_____
_____
_____

NOTES :

_____
_____
_____
_____

PUNT RETURN PLAYS:

_____
_____
_____

NOTES :

_____
_____
_____
_____

PUNT RETURN PLAYS:

NOTES :

PUNT RETURN
PLAYS:

_____
_____
_____

NOTES :
_____
_____
_____
_____

PUNT RETURN
PLAYS:

_____
_____
_____

NOTES :

_____
_____
_____
_____

PUNT RETURN PLAYS:

NOTES :

PUNT RETURN PLAYS:

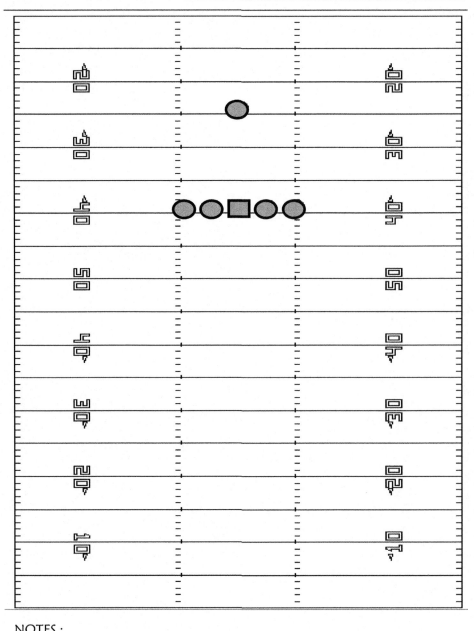

NOTES :

PUNT RETURN PLAYS:

_____
_____
_____
_____

NOTES :

_____
_____
_____
_____

PUNT RETURN
PLAYS:

_____
_____
_____

NOTES :

_____
_____
_____
_____

PUNT RETURN PLAYS:

NOTES :

PUNT RETURN PLAYS:

_____
_____
_____

NOTES :

_____
_____
_____
_____

PUNT RETURN PLAYS:

NOTES :

_____
_____
_____
_____

PUNT RETURN PLAYS:

_____
_____
_____

NOTES :

_____
_____
_____
_____

PUNT RETURN PLAYS:

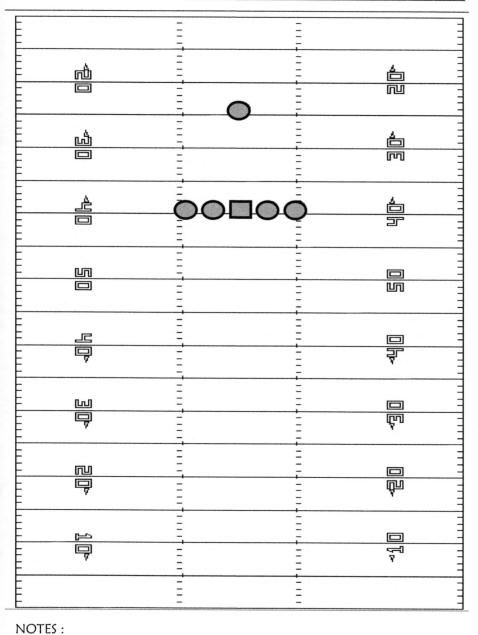

NOTES :

NOTES

4

EVALUATION FILLING IN PUNT RETURNERS

_____
_____
_____
_____
_____
_____
_____
_____
_____
_____
_____
_____
_____
_____
_____
_____
_____
_____
_____
_____
_____
_____
_____
_____
_____
_____
_____
_____

RETURNING SHEET

#	NAME	PLAYERS EVALUATION HANDS																ATT	GOOD
		1	2	3	4	5	6	7	8	9	10	11	12	13	14	15	16		
1																			
2																			
3																			
4																			
5																			
6																			

DATE _____   TOTAL _____

RETURNING SHEET

PLAYERS EVALUATION HANDS

#	NAME	1	2	3	4	5	6	7	8	9	10	11	12	13	14	15	16	ATT	GOOD
1																			
2																			
3																			
4																			
5																			
6																			

DATE _____   TOTAL _____

RETURNING SHEET

#	NAME	1	2	3	4	5	6	7	8	9	10	11	12	13	14	15	16	ATT	GOOD
1																			
2																			
3																			
4																			
5																			
6																			

PLAYERS EVALUATION HANDS

DATE _____

TOTAL _____

RETURNING SHEET

PLAYERS EVALUATION HANDS

#	NAME	1	2	3	4	5	6	7	8	9	10	11	12	13	14	15	16	ATT	GOOD
1																			
2																			
3																			
4																			
5																			
6																			

DATE

TOTAL

RETURNING SHEET

#	NAME	PLAYERS EVALUATION HANDS																ATT	GOOD
		1	2	3	4	5	6	7	8	9	10	11	12	13	14	15	16		
1																			
2																			
3																			
4																			
5																			
6																			

DATE _____   TOTAL _____

RETURNING SHEET

PLAYERS EVALUATION HANDS

#	NAME	1	2	3	4	5	6	7	8	9	10	11	12	13	14	15	16	ATT	GOOD
1																			
2																			
3																			
4																			
5																			
6																			

DATE _____   TOTAL _____

RETURNING SHEET

#	NAME	PLAYERS EVALUATION HANDS																ATT	GOOD
		1	2	3	4	5	6	7	8	9	10	11	12	13	14	15	16		
1																			
2																			
3																			
4																			
5																			
6																			

DATE _____   TOTAL _____

RETURNING SHEET

PLAYERS EVALUATION HANDS

#	NAME	1	2	3	4	5	6	7	8	9	10	11	12	13	14	15	16	ATT	GOOD
1																			
2																			
3																			
4																			
5																			
6																			

DATE _____   TOTAL _____

RETURNING SHEET

PLAYERS EVALUATION HANDS

#	NAME	1	2	3	4	5	6	7	8	9	10	11	12	13	14	15	16	ATT	GOOD
1																			
2																			
3																			
4																			
5																			
6																			

DATE _____

TOTAL _____

RETURNING SHEET

PLAYERS EVALUATION HANDS

#	NAME	1	2	3	4	5	6	7	8	9	10	11	12	13	14	15	16	ATT	GOOD
1																			
2																			
3																			
4																			
5																			
6																			

DATE _____   TOTAL _____

RETURNING SHEET

#	NAME	PLAYERS EVALUATION HANDS																ATT	GOOD
		1	2	3	4	5	6	7	8	9	10	11	12	13	14	15	16		
1																			
2																			
3																			
4																			
5																			
6																			

DATE _____   TOTAL _____

RETURNING SHEET

PLAYERS EVALUATION HANDS

#	NAME	1	2	3	4	5	6	7	8	9	10	11	12	13	14	15	16	ATT	GOOD
1																			
2																			
3																			
4																			
5																			
6																			

DATE _____   TOTAL _____

RETURNING SHEET

#	NAME	1	2	3	4	5	6	7	8	9	10	11	12	13	14	15	16	ATT	GOOD

PLAYERS EVALUATION HANDS

#	NAME																		ATT	GOOD
1																			
2																			
3																			
4																			
5																			
6																			

DATE _____   TOTAL _____

RETURNING SHEET

PLAYERS EVALUATION HANDS

# NAME	1	2	3	4	5	6	7	8	9	10	11	12	13	14	15	16	ATT	GOOD
1																		
2																		
3																		
4																		
5																		
6																		

DATE _____   TOTAL _____

RETURNING SHEET

PLAYERS EVALUATION HANDS

#	NAME	1	2	3	4	5	6	7	8	9	10	11	12	13	14	15	16	ATT	GOOD
1																			
2																			
3																			
4																			
5																			
6																			

DATE

TOTAL

RETURNING SHEET

PLAYERS EVALUATION HANDS

#	NAME	1	2	3	4	5	6	7	8	9	10	11	12	13	14	15	16	ATT	GOOD
1																			
2																			
3																			
4																			
5																			
6																			

DATE _____   TOTAL _____

RETURNING SHEET

PLAYERS EVALUATION HANDS

#	NAME	1	2	3	4	5	6	7	8	9	10	11	12	13	14	15	16	ATT	GOOD
1																			
2																			
3																			
4																			
5																			
6																			

DATE _____   TOTAL _____

RETURNING SHEET

PLAYERS EVALUATION HANDS

#	NAME	1	2	3	4	5	6	7	8	9	10	11	12	13	14	15	16	ATT	GOOD
1																			
2																			
3																			
4																			
5																			
6																			

DATE _____   TOTAL _____

RETURNING SHEET

#	NAME	1	2	3	4	5	6	7	8	9	10	11	12	13	14	15	16	ATT	GOOD
1																			
2																			
3																			
4																			
5																			
6																			

PLAYERS EVALUATION HANDS

DATE _____   TOTAL _____

RETURNING SHEET

PLAYERS EVALUATION HANDS

#	NAME	1	2	3	4	5	6	7	8	9	10	11	12	13	14	15	16	ATT	GOOD
1																			
2																			
3																			
4																			
5																			
6																			

DATE _____   TOTAL _____

RETURNING SHEET

PLAYERS EVALUATION HANDS

#	NAME	1	2	3	4	5	6	7	8	9	10	11	12	13	14	15	16	ATT	GOOD
1																			
2																			
3																			
4																			
5																			
6																			

DATE _____   TOTAL _____

RETURNING SHEET

PLAYERS EVALUATION HANDS

#	NAME	1	2	3	4	5	6	7	8	9	10	11	12	13	14	15	16	ATT	GOOD
1																			
2																			
3																			
4																			
5																			
6																			

DATE _____   TOTAL   _____

RETURNING SHEET

#	NAME	PLAYERS EVALUATION HANDS																ATT	GOOD
		1	2	3	4	5	6	7	8	9	10	11	12	13	14	15	16		
1																			
2																			
3																			
4																			
5																			
6																			

DATE _____ _____ TOTAL _____

RETURNING SHEET

PLAYERS EVALUATION HANDS

#	NAME	1	2	3	4	5	6	7	8	9	10	11	12	13	14	15	16	ATT	GOOD
1																			
2																			
3																			
4																			
5																			
6																			

DATE _____   TOTAL _____

RETURNING SHEET

NAME		PLAYERS EVALUATION HANDS																ATT	GOOD
#	1	2	3	4	5	6	7	8	9	10	11	12	13	14	15	16			
1																			
2																			
3																			
4																			
5																			
6																			

DATE _____   TOTAL _____

RETURNING SHEET

PLAYERS EVALUATION HANDS

#	NAME	1	2	3	4	5	6	7	8	9	10	11	12	13	14	15	16	ATT	GOOD
1																			
2																			
3																			
4																			
5																			
6																			

DATE _____   TOTAL _____

RETURNING SHEET

PLAYERS EVALUATION HANDS

#	NAME	1	2	3	4	5	6	7	8	9	10	11	12	13	14	15	16	ATT	GOOD
1																			
2																			
3																			
4																			
5																			
6																			

DATE _____   TOTAL _____

RETURNING SHEET

PLAYERS EVALUATION HANDS

#	NAME	1	2	3	4	5	6	7	8	9	10	11	12	13	14	15	16	ATT	GOOD
1																			
2																			
3																			
4																			
5																			
6																			

DATE _____   TOTAL _____

RETURNING SHEET

PLAYERS EVALUATION HANDS

#	NAME	1	2	3	4	5	6	7	8	9	10	11	12	13	14	15	16	ATT	GOOD
1																			
2																			
3																			
4																			
5																			
6																			

DATE _____   TOTAL _____

RETURNING SHEET

PLAYERS EVALUATION HANDS

#	NAME	1	2	3	4	5	6	7	8	9	10	11	12	13	14	15	16	ATT	GOOD
1																			
2																			
3																			
4																			
5																			
6																			

DATE _____   TOTAL _____

NOTES

5

KO PLAYS
AND ADJUSTMENTS

_____

_____

_____

_____

_____

_____

_____

_____

_____

_____

_____

_____

_____

_____

_____

_____

_____

_____

_____

_____

_____

_____

_____

_____

_____

_____

_____

_____

_____

_____

KO PLAY AND COVERAGE:

1 2 3 4 5 6 7 8 9 10
K

KO PLAY AND COVERAGE:

1 2 3 4 5 6 7 8 9 10

K

KO PLAY AND COVERAGE:

NOTES :
_____
_____

1 2 3 4 5 6 7 8 9 10

K

KO PLAY AND COVERAGE:

1 2 3 4 5 6 7 8 9 10

K

KO PLAY AND COVERAGE:

1 2 3 4 5 6 7 8 9 10

K

KO PLAY AND COVERAGE:

1 2 3 4 5 6 7 8 9 10

K

KO PLAY AND COVERAGE:

KO PLAY AND COVERAGE:

1 2 3 4 5 6 7 8 9 10

K

KO PLAY AND COVERAGE:

1 2 3 4 5 6 7 8 9 10
          K

KO PLAY AND COVERAGE:

1 2 3 4 5 6 7 8 9 10

K

KO PLAY AND COVERAGE:

KO PLAY AND COVERAGE:

1 2 3 4 5 6 7 8 9 10

K

KO PLAY AND COVERAGE:

1 2 3 4 5 6 7 8 9 10
K

KO PLAY AND
COVERAGE:

1 2 3 4 5 6 7 8 9 10

K

KO PLAY AND COVERAGE:

NOTES :
_____
_____

KO PLAY AND
COVERAGE:

KO PLAY AND COVERAGE:

1 2 3 4 5 6 7 8 9 10

K

KO PLAY AND COVERAGE:

1 2 3 4 5 6 7 8 9 10

K

KO PLAY AND COVERAGE:

1 2 3 4 5 6 7 8 9 10

K

KO PLAY AND COVERAGE:

1 2 3 4 5 6 7 8 9 10
K

NOTES

6

KO RETURN PLAYS

KO RETURN PLAYS:

NOTES :
_____
_____

1 2 3 4 5 6 7 8 9 10

K

KO RETURN PLAYS:

KO RETURN PLAYS:

1 2 3 4 5 6 7 8 9 10

K

KO RETURN PLAYS:

KO RETURN
PLAYS:

KO RETURN PLAYS:

NOTES :
_____
_____

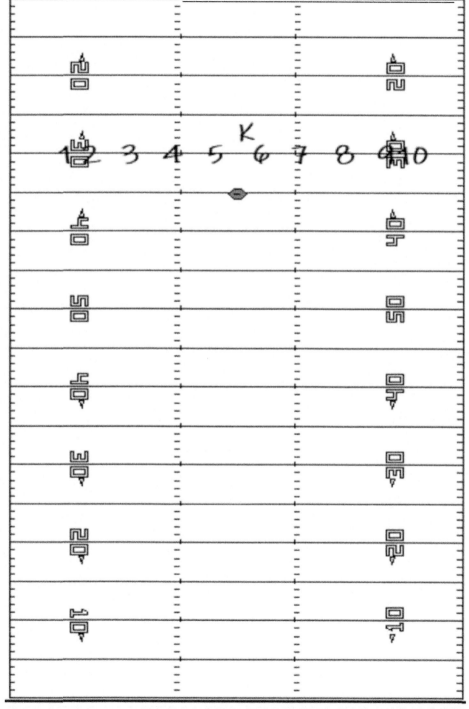

KO RETURN PLAYS:

KO RETURN
PLAYS:

KO RETURN
PLAYS:

1 2 3 4 5 K 6 7 8 9 10

KO RETURN
PLAYS:

NOTES :
_____
_____

KO RETURN
PLAYS:

NOTES :

_____

_____

1 2 3 4 5 K 6 7 8 9 10

KO RETURN PLAYS:

KO RETURN PLAYS:

KO RETURN PLAYS:

KO RETURN PLAYS:

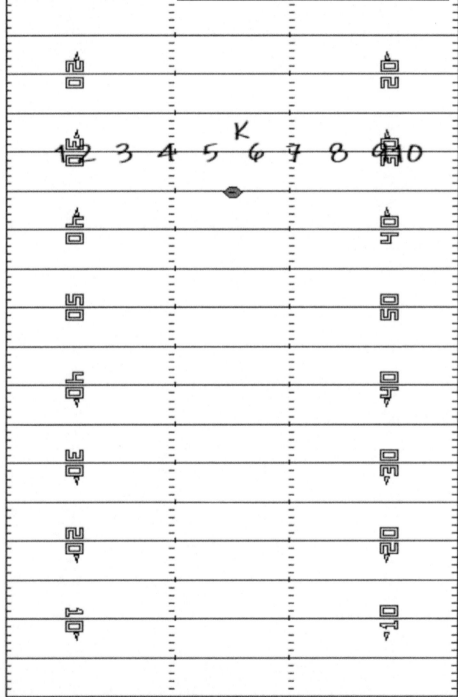

KO RETURN PLAYS:

1 2 3 4 5 **K** 6 7 8 9 10

KO RETURN PLAYS:

1 2 3 4 5 K 6 7 8 9 10

KO RETURN
PLAYS:

1 2 3 4 5 K 6 7 8 9 10

KO RETURN PLAYS:

KO RETURN
PLAYS:

NOTES

7

EVALUATION
KICKERS
FG & KO

_____
_____
_____
_____
_____
_____
_____
_____
_____
_____
_____
_____
_____
_____
_____
_____
_____
_____
_____
_____
_____
_____
_____
_____
_____
_____
_____
_____
_____

PRACTICE #

NOTES :

KICKER PRACTICE

FLEX

FG DRILL					TOTAL	
					ATT	GOOD
					12	

YD	good	YD	good	good	YD
15		15			15
20		20			20
25		25			25
30		30			30

KO DRILL				TOTAL	
				ATT	HT
				9	

30   30

HT   HT

35		35
35	HT	35
35	35	35
	35	
	35	

PRACTICE

KICKER PRACTICE
FLEX

FG DRILL							TOTAL	
							ATT	GOOD
							12	

YD	good	YD	good	good	YD
15		15			15
20		20			20
25		25			25
30		30			30

KO DRILL				TOTAL	
				ATT	HT
				9	

30

30

HT   HT

35		35
35	HT	35
35	35	35
	35	
	35	

PRACTICE

NOTES :
_____
_____

KICKER PRACTICE
FLEX

FG DRILL					TOTAL	
					ATT	GOOD
					12	

YD	good	YD	good	good	YD
15	_____	15		_____	15
20	_____	20		_____	20
25	_____	25		_____	25
30	_____	30		_____	30

KO DRILL				TOTAL	
				ATT	HT
				9	

30
30   HT   HT

35		35
35	HT	35
35	35	35
	35	
	35	

PRACTICE

NOTES :
_____
_____

KICKER PRACTICE
FLEX

FG DRILL						TOTAL	
						ATT	GOOD
						12	

YD	good	YD	good	good	YD
15	___	15	___	___	15
20	___	20	___	___	20
25	___	25	___	___	25
30	___	30	___	___	30

KO DRILL				TOTAL	
				ATT	HT
				9	

3 0   3 0

HT   HT

35		35
35	HT	35
35	35	35
	35	
	35	

PRACTICE

NOTES :
_____
_____

KICKER PRACTICE
FLEX

FG DRILL					TOTAL	
					ATT	GOOD
					12	

YD	good	YD	good	good	YD	
15	___	15	___	___	15	
20	___	20	___	___	20	
25	___	25	___	___	25	
30	___	30	___	___	30	

KO DRILL			TOTAL	
			ATT	HT
			9	

30

30

HT   HT

35			35
35		HT	35
35	35		35
	35		
	35		

PRACTICE #

KICKER PRACTICE
FLEX

FG DRILL

	TOTAL	
	ATT	GOOD
	12	

YD	good	YD	good	good	YD
15	___	15		___	15
20	___	20		___	20
25	___	25		___	25
30	___	30		___	30

KO DRILL

	TOTAL	
	ATT	HT
	9	

30

30

HT   HT

35		35
35	HT	35
35	35	35
	35	
	35	

PRACTICE

NOTES :
_____
_____

KICKER PRACTICE
FLEX

FG DRILL					TOTAL	
					ATT	GOOD
					12	

YD	good	YD	good	good	YD
15	___	15		___	15
20	___	20		___	20
25	___	25		___	25
30	___	30		___	30

KO DRILL					TOTAL	
					ATT	HT
					9	

3 0			3 0
	HT	HT	
35 ___			35 ___
35 ___	HT		35 ___
35 ___	35		35 ___
	35 ___		
	35 ___		

PRACTICE #

_____
_____

KICKER PRACTICE
FLEX

FG DRILL						TOTAL	
						ATT	GOOD
						12	

YD	good	YD	good	good	YD
15	___	15		___	15
20	___	20		___	20
25	___	25		___	25
30	___	30		___	30

KO DRILL				TOTAL	
				ATT	HT
				9	

3 0			3 0
HT		HT	
35		35	
35	HT	35	
35	35	35	
	35		
	35		

PRACTICE

KICKER PRACTICE

FLEX

FG DRILL			TOTAL	
			ATT	GOOD
			12	

YD	good	YD	good	good	YD
15		15			15
20		20			20
25		25			25
30		30			30

KO DRILL			TOTAL	
			ATT	HT
			9	

30

30

HT   HT

35		35
35	HT	35
35	35	35
	35	
	35	

PRACTICE

NOTES :
_____
_____

KICKER PRACTICE
FLEX

FG DRILL			TOTAL	
			ATT	GOOD
			12	

YD	good	YD	good	good	YD
15	___	15	___	___	15
20	___	20	___	___	20
25	___	25	___	___	25
30	___	30	___	___	30

KO DRILL		TOTAL	
		ATT	HT
		9	

30   30

HT   HT

35		35
35	HT	35
35	35	35
	35	
	35	

PRACTICE #

_____

_____

KICKER PRACTICE

FLEX

FG DRILL							TOTAL	
							ATT	GOOD
							12	

YD	good	YD	good	good	YD
15	____	15			15
20	____	20			20
25	____	25			25
30	____	30			30

KO DRILL				TOTAL	
				ATT	HT
				9	

30			30
HT		HT	
35			35
35	HT		35
35	35		35
	35		
	35		

PRACTICE

NOTES :
_____
_____

KICKER PRACTICE
FLEX

FG DRILL

	TOTAL	
	ATT	GOOD
	12	

YD	good	YD	good	good	YD
15	____	15		____	15
20	____	20		____	20
25	____	25		____	25
30	____	30		____	30

KO DRILL

	TOTAL	
	ATT	HT
	9	

30
30

HT   HT

35		35
35	HT	35
35	35	35
	35	
	35	

PRACTICE

NOTES :

KICKER PRACTICE

FLEX

FG DRILL				TOTAL	
				ATT	GOOD
				12	

YD	good	YD	good	good	YD
15		15			15
20		20			20
25		25			25
30		30			30

KO DRILL				TOTAL	
				ATT	HT
				9	

30

30

HT   HT

35	HT	35
35		35
35	35	35
	35	
	35	

NOTES :
_____
_____

KICKER PRACTICE
FLEX

FG DRILL						TOTAL	
						ATT	GOOD
						12	

YD	good	YD	good	good	YD
15	___	15	___		15
20	___	20	___		20
25	___	25	___		25
30	___	30	___		30

KO DRILL						TOTAL	
						ATT	HT
						9	

30   30

HT   HT

35		35
35	HT	35
35	35	35
	35	
	35	

PRACTICE

KICKER PRACTICE

FLEX

FG DRILL							TOTAL	
							ATT	GOOD
							12	

YD	good		YD	good		good	YD	
15			15				15	
20			20				20	
25			25				25	
30			30				30	

KO DRILL						TOTAL	
						ATT	HT
						9	

3 0   3 0

HT   HT

35			35
35	HT		35
35	35		35
	35		
	35		

PRACTICE #

_____
_____

KICKER PRACTICE
FLEX

FG DRILL						TOTAL	
						ATT	GOOD
						12	

YD	good	YD	good	good	YD
15	___	15	___	___	15
20	___	20	___	___	20
25	___	25	___	___	25
30	___	30	___	___	30

KO DRILL					TOTAL	
					ATT	HT
					9	

3 0   3 0

HT   HT

35	___		35	___
35		HT	35	
35		35	35	
		35		
		35		

NOTES :
_____
_____

KICKER PRACTICE
FLEX

FG DRILL						TOTAL	
						ATT	GOOD
						12	

YD	good	YD	good	good	YD
15	___	15		___	15
20	___	20		___	20
25	___	25		___	25
30	___	30		___	30

KO DRILL						TOTAL	
						ATT	HT
						9	

30

30

HT   HT

35		35
35	HT	35
35	35	35
	35	
	35	

PRACTICE #

_____
_____

KICKER PRACTICE
FLEX

FG DRILL						TOTAL	
						ATT	GOOD
						12	

YD	good	YD	good	good	YD
15	____	15		____	15
20	____	20		____	20
25	____	25		____	25
30	____	30		____	30

KO DRILL				TOTAL	
				ATT	HT
				9	

30   30

HT   HT

35		35
35	HT	35
35	35	35
	35	
	35	

PRACTICE

NOTES :

KICKER PRACTICE
FLEX

FG DRILL					TOTAL	
					ATT	GOOD
					12	

YD	good	YD	good	good	YD
15	___	15			15
20	___	20			20
25	___	25			25
30	___	30			30

KO DRILL			TOTAL	
			ATT	HT
			9	

30
30

HT   HT

35		35
35	HT	35
35	35	35
	35	
	35	

PRACTICE

NOTES :
_____
_____

KICKER PRACTICE
FLEX

FG DRILL					TOTAL	
					ATT	GOOD
					12	

YD	good	YD	good	good	YD
15	____	15		____	15
20	____	20		____	20
25	____	25		____	25
30	____	30		____	30

KO DRILL			TOTAL	
			ATT	HT
			9	

30
0

30

HT

HT

35	____		35	
35	____	HT	35	
35	____	35	35	
		35		
		35		

PRACTICE

KICKER PRACTICE

FLEX

FG DRILL					TOTAL	
					ATT	GOOD
					12	

YD	good	YD	good	good	YD
15		15			15
20		20			20
25		25			25
30		30			30

KO DRILL					TOTAL	
					ATT	HT
					9	

30

30

HT   HT

35		35
35	HT	35
35	35	35
	35	
	35	

PRACTICE #

KICKER PRACTICE
FLEX

FG DRILL				TOTAL	
				ATT	GOOD
				12	

YD	good	YD	good	good	YD
15		15			15
20		20			20
25		25			25
30		30			30

KO DRILL			TOTAL	
			ATT	HT
			9	

30   30

HT   HT

35		35
35	HT	35
35	35	35
	35	
	35	

PRACTICE

NOTES :
_____
_____

KICKER PRACTICE
FLEX

FG DRILL						TOTAL	
						ATT	GOOD
						12	

	YD	good	YD	good	good	YD	
	15	___	15		___	15	
	20	___	20		___	20	
	25	___	25		___	25	
	30	___	30		___	30	

KO DRILL					TOTAL	
					ATT	HT
					9	

30   30

HT   HT

35		35
35	HT	35
35	35	35
	35	
	35	

PRACTICE #

KICKER PRACTICE
FLEX

FG DRILL				TOTAL	
				ATT	GOOD
				12	

YD	good	YD	good	good	YD
15	____	15	____		15
20	____	20	____		20
25	____	25	____		25
30	____	30	____		30

KO DRILL			TOTAL	
			ATT	HT
			9	

30
30

HT

30
30

HT

35		35
35	HT	35
35	35	35
	35	
	35	

PRACTICE #

KICKER PRACTICE

FLEX

FG DRILL					TOTAL	
					ATT	GOOD
					12	

YD	good	YD	good	good	YD
15	___	15		___	15
20	___	20		___	20
25	___	25		___	25
30	___	30		___	30

KO DRILL					TOTAL	
					ATT	HT
					9	

30

30

HT   HT

35		35
35	HT	35
35	35	35
	35	
	35	

NOTES :
_____
_____

KICKER PRACTICE
FLEX

FG DRILL						TOTAL	
						ATT	GOOD
						12	

YD	good	YD	good	good	YD
15	___	15	___	___	15
20	___	20	___	___	20
25	___	25	___	___	25
30	___	30	___	___	30

KO DRILL					TOTAL	
					ATT	HT
					9	

3 0

3 0

HT   HT

35		35
35	HT	35
35	35	35
	35	
	35	

PRACTICE

NOTES :
_____
_____

KICKER PRACTICE
FLEX

FG DRILL					TOTAL	
					ATT	GOOD
					12	

YD	good	YD	good	good	YD
15	___	15			15
20	___	20			20
25	___	25			25
30	___	30			30

KO DRILL			TOTAL	
			ATT	HT
			9	

30			30
	HT	HT	
35			35
35	HT		35
35	35		35
	35		
	35		

PRACTICE

KICKER PRACTICE
FLEX

FG DRILL					TOTAL	
					ATT	GOOD
					12	

YD	good	YD	good	good	YD	
15	___	15		___	15	
20	___	20		___	20	
25	___	25		___	25	
30	___	30		___	30	

KO DRILL			TOTAL	
			ATT	HT
			9	

30
30

HT   HT

35		35
35	HT	35
35	35	35
	35	
	35	

PRACTICE #

KICKER PRACTICE
FLEX

FG DRILL							TOTAL	
							ATT	GOOD
							12	

YD	good	YD	good	good	YD
15		15			15
20		20			20
25		25			25
30		30			30

KO DRILL						TOTAL	
						ATT	HT
						9	

30   30

HT   HT

35		35
35	HT	35
35	35	35
	35	
	35	

PRACTICE #

KICKER PRACTICE

FLEX

FG DRILL				TOTAL	
				ATT	GOOD
				12	

YD	good	YD	good	good	YD
15	___	15		___	15
20	___	20		___	20
25	___	25		___	25
30	___	30			30

KO DRILL				TOTAL	
				ATT	HT
				9	

3 0   3 0

HT   HT

35		35
35	HT	35
35	35	35
	35	
	35	

NOTES

8

EVALUATION
KICKERS
PUNT & 120

_____
_____
_____
_____
_____
_____
_____
_____
_____
_____
_____
_____
_____
_____
_____
_____
_____
_____
_____
_____
_____
_____
_____
_____
_____
_____
_____
_____
_____
_____
_____
_____
_____
_____
_____

PRACTICE #

NOTES :
_____
_____

| KICKER PRACTICE |
| FLEX |

PUNT	50	🏈	50	TOTAL	
				ATT	HT
				8	

YD HT   HT YD

____ ____   ____ ____

____ ____   ____ ____

____ ____   ____ ____

____   K   ____

120			TOTAL	
			ATT	GOOD
			8	

🏈   🏈

10   10

good   good

ATT ____   ____ ATT
ATT ____   ____ ATT
ATT ____   ____ ATT
ATT ____   ____ ATT

PRACTICE #

KICKER PRACTICE
FLEX

PUNT	50	🏈	50	TOTAL	
				ATT	HT
				8	

YD　HT　　　　　　　　HT **YD**

_____　　_____

_____　　_____

_____　　_____

_____　　K　　_____

120				TOTAL	
				ATT	GOOD
				8	

🏈 **10**　　　　　🏈 **10**

good　　　　　　　　　　good

ATT _____　　　　　　　　_____ ATT

ATT _____　　　　　　　　_____ ATT

ATT _____　　　　　　　　_____ ATT

ATT _____　　　　　　　　_____ ATT

PRACTICE

NOTES :
_____
_____

KICKER PRACTICE
FLEX

PUNT	50	🏈	50	TOTAL	
				ATT	HT
				8	

YD   HT   HT YD

_____   _____

_____   _____

_____   _____

K

_____   _____

120				TOTAL	
				ATT	GOOD
				8	

10   10

good   good

ATT _____   _____ ATT

ATT _____   _____ ATT

ATT _____   _____ ATT

ATT _____   _____ ATT

PRACTICE #

KICKER PRACTICE
FLEX

PUNT	50	🏈	50	TOTAL	
				ATT	HT
				8	

	YD HT		HT YD	
	___		___	
	___		___	
	___	K	___	
	___		___	

120				TOTAL	
				ATT	GOOD
				8	

🏈 10	🏈 10
good	good
ATT ___	___ ATT
ATT ___	___ ATT
ATT ___	___ ATT
ATT ___	___ ATT

PRACTICE

KICKER PRACTICE

FLEX

PUNT	50	🏈	50	TOTAL	
				ATT	HT
				8	

YD	HT		HT	YD
___	___		___	___
___	___		___	___
___	___	K	___	___
___			___	

I20			TOTAL	
			ATT	GOOD
			8	

🏈 10   🏈 10

good   good

ATT	___		___	ATT
ATT	___		___	ATT
ATT	___		___	ATT
ATT	___		___	ATT

PRACTICE #

KICKER PRACTICE
FLEX

PUNT	50	🏈	50	TOTAL	
				ATT	HT
				8	

YD HT   HT **YD**

_____   _____

_____   _____

_____   _____

_____   **K**   _____

120			TOTAL	
			ATT	GOOD
			8	

🏈 10   🏈 10

good   good

ATT _____   _____ ATT

ATT _____   _____ ATT

ATT _____   _____ ATT

ATT _____   _____ ATT

PRACTICE

NOTES :
_____
_____

KICKER PRACTICE
FLEX

PUNT	50		50	TOTAL	
				ATT	HT
				8	

YD HT   HT YD

_____   _____

_____   _____

_____   _____

_____   K   _____

120				TOTAL	
				ATT	GOOD
				8	

10		10

good   good

ATT _____   _____ ATT

ATT _____   _____ ATT

ATT _____   _____ ATT

ATT _____   _____ ATT

PRACTICE

KICKER PRACTICE

FLEX

PUNT	50	🏈	50	TOTAL	
				ATT	HT
				8	

YD HT   HT YD

_____   _____

_____   _____

_____   _____

K

_____   _____

120				TOTAL	
				ATT	GOOD
				8	

🏈 10   🏈 10

good   good

ATT _____   _____ ATT

ATT _____   _____ ATT

ATT _____   _____ ATT

ATT _____   _____ ATT

PRACTICE #

NOTES :
_____
_____

| KICKER PRACTICE |
| FLEX |

PUNT	50	🏈	50	TOTAL	
				ATT	HT
				8	

YD　HT　　　　　　　　HT　YD

___　　　　　　___
___　　　　　　___
___　　　　　　___
___　　　K　　　___

120		TOTAL	
		ATT	GOOD
		8	

🏈　　　　　　　　　🏈

| 10 | | 10 |

　good　　　　　　　　　　　good

ATT _____　　　　　　_____ ATT
ATT _____　　　　　　_____ ATT
ATT _____　　　　　　_____ ATT
ATT _____　　　　　　_____ ATT

PRACTICE #

KICKER PRACTICE
FLEX

PUNT	50	🏈	50	TOTAL	
				ATT	HT
				8	

YD HT   HT **YD**

_____   _____
_____   _____
_____   _____
_____   K   _____

120				TOTAL	
				ATT	GOOD
				8	

🏈   🏈
10   10

good   good

ATT _____   _____ ATT
ATT _____   _____ ATT
ATT _____   _____ ATT
ATT _____   _____ ATT

PRACTICE #

NOTES :
_____
_____

KICKER PRACTICE
FLEX

PUNT				TOTAL	
	50		50	ATT	HT
				8	

	YD HT		HT YD	
	___		___	
	___		___	
	___		___	
	___	K	___	

120			TOTAL	
			ATT	GOOD
			8	

10		10	
good		good	

ATT	___		___	ATT
ATT	___		___	ATT
ATT	___		___	ATT
ATT	___		___	ATT

PRACTICE

NOTES :
_____
_____

KICKER PRACTICE
FLEX

PUNT	50		50	TOTAL	
				ATT	HT
				8	

YD HT   HT YD

___   ___

___   ___

___   ___

K

___   ___

120			TOTAL	
			ATT	GOOD
			8	

10   10

good   good

ATT _____   _____ ATT

ATT _____   _____ ATT

ATT _____   _____ ATT

ATT _____   _____ ATT

PRACTICE #

KICKER PRACTICE

FLEX

PUNT	50	🏈	50	TOTAL	
				ATT	HT
				8	

YD HT   HT YD

_____   _____

_____   _____

_____   _____

_____   K   _____

120			TOTAL	
			ATT	GOOD
			8	

🏈   🏈

10		10

good   good

ATT _____   _____ ATT

ATT _____   _____ ATT

ATT _____   _____ ATT

ATT _____   _____ ATT

NOTES :
_____
_____

KICKER PRACTICE
FLEX

PUNT	50	🏈	50	TOTAL	
				ATT	HT
				8	

YD HT   HT **YD**

_____   _____

_____   _____

_____   _____

_____   K   _____

120			TOTAL	
			ATT	GOOD
			8	

🏈 10   🏈 10

good   good

ATT _____   _____ ATT

ATT _____   _____ ATT

ATT _____   _____ ATT

ATT _____   _____ ATT

PRACTICE

NOTES :
_____
_____

KICKER PRACTICE
FLEX

PUNT	50	🏈	50	TOTAL	
				ATT	HT
				8	

	YD HT		HT YD		
	___		___		
	___		___		
	___		___		
	___	K	___		

120				TOTAL	
				ATT	GOOD
				8	

🏈 10		🏈 10	
good		good	
ATT ___		___ ATT	
ATT ___		___ ATT	
ATT ___		___ ATT	
ATT ___		___ ATT	

PRACTICE #

_____
_____

KICKER PRACTICE
FLEX

PUNT	50	🏈	50	TOTAL	
				ATT	HT
				8	

YD HT   HT YD

___   ___

___   ___

___   ___

___   K   ___

120				TOTAL	
				ATT	GOOD
				8	

🏈   🏈

| 10 | | 10 |

good   good

ATT ___   ___ ATT

ATT ___   ___ ATT

ATT ___   ___ ATT

ATT ___   ___ ATT

PRACTICE

NOTES :

_____

_____

KICKER PRACTICE

FLEX

PUNT	50		50	TOTAL	
				ATT	HT
				8	

YD   HT   HT YD

_____   _____

_____   _____

_____   _____

_____   K   _____

120		TOTAL	
		ATT	GOOD
		8	

10   10

good   good

ATT _____   _____ ATT

ATT _____   _____ ATT

ATT _____   _____ ATT

ATT _____   _____ ATT

PRACTICE #

_____

_____

KICKER PRACTICE
FLEX

PUNT	50	🏈	50	TOTAL	
				ATT	HT
				8	

YD   HT   HT YD

_____   _____

_____   _____

_____   _____

_____   K   _____

120				TOTAL	
				ATT	GOOD
				8	

🏈 10   🏈 10

good   good

ATT _____   _____ ATT

ATT _____   _____ ATT

ATT _____   _____ ATT

ATT _____   _____ ATT

PRACTICE

NOTES : _____
_____

KICKER PRACTICE
FLEX

PUNT	50	🏈	50	TOTAL	
				ATT	HT
				8	

YD   HT   HT YD

_____   _____
_____   _____
_____   _____
_____   K   _____

120				TOTAL	
				ATT	GOOD
				8	

🏈 10   🏈 10

good   good

ATT _____   _____ ATT
ATT _____   _____ ATT
ATT _____   _____ ATT
ATT _____   _____ ATT

PRACTICE #

NOTES :

KICKER PRACTICE
FLEX

PUNT	50		50	TOTAL	
				ATT	HT
				8	

YD HT   HT YD

K

120				TOTAL	
				ATT	GOOD
				8	

10			10

good   good

ATT ____   ____ ATT
ATT ____   ____ ATT
ATT ____   ____ ATT
ATT ____   ____ ATT

PRACTICE #

KICKER PRACTICE

FLEX

PUNT	50	🏈	50	TOTAL	
				ATT	HT
				8	

	YD	HT		HT	YD	
	___	___		___	___	
	___	___		___	___	
	___	___		___	___	
	___	___	K	___	___	

120			TOTAL	
			ATT	GOOD
			8	

10		10
good		good

ATT	_____		_____	ATT
ATT	_____		_____	ATT
ATT	_____		_____	ATT
ATT	_____		_____	ATT

PRACTICE #

KICKER PRACTICE

FLEX

PUNT	50	🏈	50	TOTAL	
				ATT	HT
				8	

YD HT   HT YD

_____   _____

_____   _____

_____   _____

_____   K   _____

120			TOTAL	
			ATT	GOOD
			8	

🏈   🏈

| 10 | | 10 |

good   good

ATT _____   _____ ATT

ATT _____   _____ ATT

ATT _____   _____ ATT

ATT _____   _____ ATT

PRACTICE

NOTES :
_____
_____

KICKER PRACTICE
FLEX

PUNT	50	🏈	50	TOTAL	
				ATT	HT
				8	

YD   HT   HT **YD**

_____   _____

_____   _____

_____   _____

_____   K   _____

120				TOTAL	
				ATT	GOOD
				8	

🏈 | 10 | 🏈 | 10 |

good   *good*

ATT	_____			_____	ATT
ATT	_____			_____	ATT
ATT	_____			_____	ATT
ATT	_____			_____	ATT

PRACTICE #

KICKER PRACTICE
FLEX

PUNT	50	🏈	50	TOTAL	
				ATT	HT
				8	

YD   HT   HT YD

_____   _____

_____   _____

_____   _____

_____   **K**   _____

120				TOTAL	
				ATT	GOOD
				8	

🏈   🏈

10		10

good   good

ATT _____   _____ ATT

ATT _____   _____ ATT

ATT _____   _____ ATT

ATT _____   _____ ATT

PRACTICE #

KICKER PRACTICE

FLEX

PUNT	50	🏈	50	TOTAL	
				ATT	HT
				8	

YD　HT　　　　　　　　HT YD

___　　　　　　　　___

___　　　　　　　　___

___　　　　　　　　___

___　　　K　　　___

120				TOTAL	
				ATT	GOOD
				8	

10		10

good　　　　　　　　　　*good*

ATT _____　　　　　　　　_____ ATT

ATT _____　　　　　　　　_____ ATT

ATT _____　　　　　　　　_____ ATT

ATT _____　　　　　　　　_____ ATT

PRACTICE #

NOTES :
_____
_____

KICKER PRACTICE
FLEX

PUNT	50		50	TOTAL	
				ATT	HT
				8	

YD   HT   HT **YD**

_____   _____
_____   _____
_____   _____
_____   K   _____

120				TOTAL	
				ATT	GOOD
				8	

10   10

good   good

ATT _____   _____ ATT
ATT _____   _____ ATT
ATT _____   _____ ATT
ATT _____   _____ ATT

PRACTICE

_____
_____

KICKER PRACTICE
FLEX

PUNT				TOTAL	
	50		50	ATT	HT
				8	

YD HT   HT YD

_____   _____
_____   _____
_____   _____
_____   K   _____

120			TOTAL	
			ATT	GOOD
			8	

10		10
good		good

ATT	_____		_____	ATT
ATT	_____		_____	ATT
ATT	_____		_____	ATT
ATT	_____		_____	ATT

PRACTICE #

KICKER PRACTICE
FLEX

PUNT	50		50	TOTAL	
				ATT	HT
				8	

YD HT   HT YD

_____   _____
_____   _____
_____   _____

K

_____   _____

I20			TOTAL	
			ATT	GOOD
			8	

10		10

good   good

ATT _____   _____ ATT
ATT _____   _____ ATT
ATT _____   _____ ATT
ATT _____   _____ ATT

PRACTICE #

KICKER PRACTICE

FLEX

PUNT	50	🏈	50	TOTAL	
				ATT	HT
				8	

YD   HT   HT YD

———   ———

———   ———

———   ———

———   K   ———

120				TOTAL	
				ATT	GOOD
				8	

🏈   🏈

10		10

good   good

ATT ———   ——— ATT

ATT ———   ——— ATT

ATT ———   ——— ATT

ATT ———   ——— ATT

PRACTICE #

NOTES :

_____

_____

KICKER PRACTICE
FLEX

PUNT	50	🏈	50	TOTAL	
				ATT	HT
				8	

YD HT   HT YD

_____   _____

_____   _____

_____   _____

_____   K   _____

120				TOTAL	
				ATT	GOOD
				8	

🏈 10   🏈 10

good   good

ATT _____   _____ ATT

ATT _____   _____ ATT

ATT _____   _____ ATT

ATT _____   _____ ATT

NOTES

9

DRAWING
FG PLAYS

_____
_____
_____
_____
_____
_____
_____
_____
_____
_____
_____
_____
_____
_____
_____
_____
_____
_____
_____
_____
_____
_____
_____
_____
_____
_____
_____
_____
_____

FG

PLAYS:

NOTES :

FG

PLAYS: _____

_____

_____

NOTES : _____

_____
_____
_____
_____
_____
_____
_____
_____

FG

PLAYS:

NOTES :

FG

PLAYS:

_____

_____

_____

NOTES :

_____

_____

_____

_____

_____

_____

_____

_____

_____

_____

FG

PLAYS:

_____
_____
_____

NOTES :

_____
_____
_____
_____
_____
_____
_____
_____
_____

FG

PLAYS: _____
_____
_____

NOTES : _____
_____
_____
_____
_____
_____
_____
_____
_____
_____

FG

PLAYS:

NOTES :

FG

PLAYS: _____
_____
_____

NOTES : _____
_____
_____
_____
_____
_____
_____
_____
_____
_____

FG

PLAYS: _____
_____
_____

NOTES :

_____
_____
_____
_____
_____
_____
_____
_____
_____
_____

FG

PLAYS: _____

NOTES :

_____
_____
_____
_____
_____
_____
_____
_____
_____

FG

PLAYS:

NOTES :

FG

PLAYS:
_____
_____
_____

NOTES :
_____
_____
_____
_____
_____
_____
_____
_____
_____

FG

PLAYS: _____
       _____

NOTES :

_____
_____
_____
_____
_____
_____
_____
_____
_____

FG

PLAYS: _____
_____
_____

-10
0

-20
0

1-0
1

2-0
2

NOTES :
_____
_____
_____
_____
_____
_____
_____
_____
_____

FG

PLAYS:

_____
_____
_____

NOTES :

_____
_____
_____
_____
_____
_____
_____
_____
_____

FG

PLAYS:
_____
_____
_____

NOTES :
_____
_____
_____
_____
_____
_____
_____
_____
_____

FG

PLAYS: _____
_____
_____

NOTES :
_____
_____
_____
_____
_____
_____
_____
_____
_____

FG
PLAYS:

_____
_____
_____

NOTES :

_____
_____
_____
_____
_____
_____
_____
_____
_____

FG

PLAYS: _____
_____
_____

NOTES : _____
_____
_____
_____
_____
_____
_____
_____
_____
_____

FG

PLAYS:

_____

_____

_____

NOTES :

_____

_____

_____

_____

_____

_____

_____

_____

_____

_____

NOTES

10

DRAWING
FG BLOCK PLAYS

FG BLOCK PLAYS:

_____
_____
_____

NOTES :
_____
_____
_____
_____
_____
_____
_____
_____
_____

FG BLOCK PLAYS:

NOTES :

FG BLOCK PLAYS:

NOTES :

FG BLOCK PLAYS: _____

NOTES :

_____
_____
_____
_____
_____
_____
_____
_____
_____

FG BLOCK PLAYS:

NOTES :

FG BLOCK PLAYS:

NOTES :

FG BLOCK PLAYS: _____

NOTES : _____

FG BLOCK PLAYS:

_____
_____
_____

NOTES :

_____
_____
_____
_____
_____
_____
_____
_____
_____

FG BLOCK PLAYS:

_____
_____
_____

NOTES :
_____
_____
_____
_____
_____
_____
_____
_____
_____

FG BLOCK PLAYS:

_____
_____
_____

NOTES :

_____
_____
_____
_____
_____
_____
_____
_____
_____
_____

FG BLOCK PLAYS:

NOTES :

FG BLOCK PLAYS:

NOTES :

FG BLOCK PLAYS:

NOTES :

FG BLOCK PLAYS:

NOTES :

FG BLOCK PLAYS:

NOTES :

FG BLOCK PLAYS: _____

NOTES : _____

FG BLOCK PLAYS:

_____
_____
_____

NOTES :

_____
_____
_____
_____
_____
_____
_____
_____
_____

FG BLOCK PLAYS:

NOTES :

FG BLOCK PLAYS: _____

NOTES : _____

FG BLOCK PLAYS:

_____

_____

_____

NOTES :

_____

_____

_____

_____

_____

_____

_____

_____

_____

FOOTBALL TEMPLATES
SPECIAL TEAMS

It comes to an end with the aim of ensuring support for quality planning and control within all the activities of a football team, serving as working tool for all coaches.

I hope you like the content of this book and can be useful to your team.

ABOUT THE AUTHOR

Hi, I´m:

Coach Javier Adame creator of the
FORCE BOOKS Project.
And as a freelance writer, I have developed
this books series, covering topics of
philosophy, principles, values, and aspects
related to football techniques and systems.

I am currently training professional
football, maintaining the idea of being
constant support for the current and new
generations.

Thank you...

For more information please contact the following email:

coachadame@hotmail.com

Subscribe to Spanish YouTube channel:

UN EQUIPO FORCE

And follow us on Instagram: **hcfootballforce**

Where you will find news regarding this collection of books.

Printed in Great Britain
by Amazon

87230566R00147